HISTORY'S MOST INFLUENTIAL WRITERS

FROM THE Late 1700s TO THE Early 1800s

William Wordsworth to Emily Brontë

EDITED BY J.E. LUEBERING

Britannica Educational Publishing
IN ASSOCIATION WITH
ROSEN
EDUCATIONAL SERVICES

Published in 2025 by Britannica Educational Publishing
(a trademark of Encyclopædia Britannica, Inc.)
in association with Rosen Educational Services, LLC
2544 Clinton Street, Buffalo, NY 14224.

Distributed exclusively by Rosen Educational Services.
For a listing of additional Britannica Educational Publishing titles, call toll free (800) 237-9932.

First Edition

Britannica Educational Publishing
Michael I. Levy: Executive Editor
Marilyn L. Barton: Senior Coordinator, Production Control
Steven Bosco: Director, Editorial Technologies
Lisa S. Braucher: Senior Producer and Data Editor
Yvette Charboneau: Senior Copy Editor
Kathy Nakamura: Manager, Media Acquisition
J. E. Luebering: Manager and Senior Editor, Literature

Editor: Greg Roza
Book design: Michael Flynn

Photo credits: Cover https://commons.wikimedia.org/wiki; pp. 10, 40 Everett Collection/Shutterstock.com; p. 17 https://commons.wikimedia.org/wiki/File:J._Austen_LCCN91783775.jpg; p. 27 https://commons.wikimedia.org/wiki/File:John_Keats,_portrait_by_Joseph_Severn.jpg; p. 35 Stocksnapper/Shutterstock.com; p. 45 https://commons.wikimedia.org/wiki/File:Charles_Dickens_circa_1860s.png; p. 51 https://commons.wikimedia.org/wiki/File:Charlotte_Bronte_by_George_Richmond.jpg.

Cataloging-in-Publication Data

Names: Luebering, J.E.
Title: From the late 1700s to the early 1800s: William Wordsworth to Emily Brontë / edited by J.E. Luebering.
Description: New York : Britannica Educational Publishing, in Association with Rosen Educational Services, 2025. | Series: History's most influential writers | Includes glossary and index.
Identifiers: ISBN 9781641901208 (library bound) | ISBN 9781641901192 (pbk) | ISBN 9781641901215 (ebook)
Subjects: LCSH: Authors--18th century--Biography. | Literature, Modern--18th century--Bio-bibliography. | Authorship--History--18th century.
Classification: LCC PN451.F766 2025 | DDC 809'.03 B --dc23

Manufactured in the United States of America

CPSIA Compliance Information: Batch #CSBRIT25. For further information contact Rosen Publishing at 1-800-237-9932.

CONTENTS

Introduction

"But this I know; the writer who possesses the creative gift owns something of which he is not always master—something that at times strangely wills and works for itself."
—Charlotte Brontë (1816–1855)

Open a book—any book. In it you'll find words, of course, but look closely and you'll also find art, crafted, in detail, by a writer proud enough to sign his or her name to the work. In a book, or in any piece of writing, words are joined together at the whim of the author. Sentences are created, paragraphs and stanzas formatted, chapters built, and stories told. In a book or a poem, a play or a short story, everything is there, on the page, for a reason: To show, to tell, to convey a message. Most works of writing, quite simply, are meant for reading. The great ones, however, by the most talented and ingenious authors, are for study. In such works, it's the art one finds within that sets them apart from the rest.

Writers are influenced by the places in which they live and the cultures in which they are steeped. The writers in this volume lived during the late 1700s or early 1800s. Many of the individuals included, such as Jane Austen, Charles Dickens, and Charlotte and Emily Brontë, are paradigms of English literature. Aleksandr Sergeyevich Pushkin, a Russian writer of the early 1800s, is a founder of modern literature in that country.

As the title of this book indicates, all those featured in this collection are influential. Through their work, they've reached out to the masses, touched the hearts and souls of millions, and left their mark on the world. Perhaps a writer's influence is determined by timeless prominence, the ability to remain relevant hundreds of years after initial publication. Several of the authors in this book fit that bill, particularly Jane Austen. Her penned explorations of everyday life in middle-class England are timeless classics primarily because her characters have many of the same foibles, and become embroiled in many of the same situations, as contemporary citizens the world over in the present day.

Not only are Austen's books required reading in many school curriculums, but the author's works have permeated modern culture in a way she never could have predicted. Movies and television miniseries based on her novels have proved quite successful, and groups dedicated to the reading and discussion of Austen's work are virtually everywhere; national and regional chapters of the Jane Austen Society dot the globe. Several authors have paid homage to Austen by writing fictionalized accounts of her life or using the themes and style of her novels as the inspiration for their own narratives. This ability to sway audiences so deeply, and in so many ways, a century or more after the fact is arguably the very definition of influential.

The truth is, influence can mean so many things and can be measured in so many ways. Those who read the works of any of the writers profiled in this book may very well discover an experience they've perhaps never had before. They might have their imagination sparked and be transported, however briefly, from the travails of the life they're living. An author's writing might, with its insight, highlight an injustice, leading readers to speak out themselves and demand an equitable resolution. Whatever the case, one can't read a work by authors such as those detailed here without being influenced in some way. That's the power of great writing. And that's the real reason we read.

WILLIAM WORDSWORTH

(b. April 7, 1770, Cockermouth, Cumberland, Eng.—d. April 23, 1850, Rydal Mount, Westmorland)

William Wordsworth was an English poet whose *Lyrical Ballads* (1798), written with Samuel Taylor Coleridge, helped launch the English Romantic movement.

Wordsworth, orphaned at age 13, entered St. John's College, Cambridge in 1787. Repelled by the competitive pressures there, he elected to idle his way through the university. The most important thing he did in his college years was to devote his summer vacation in 1790 to a long walking tour through revolutionary France. There he was caught up in the passionate enthusiasm that followed the fall of the Bastille and became an ardent republican sympathizer.

After graduation and another brief trip to France, Wordsworth found himself unprepared for any profession, rootless, virtually penniless, and bitterly hostile to his own country's opposition to the French. He lived in London in the company of radicals like William Godwin and learned to feel a profound sympathy for the abandoned mothers, beggars, children, vagrants, and victims of England's wars who began to march through the somber poems he began writing at this time. This dark period ended in 1795, when a friend's legacy made possible Wordsworth's reunion with his beloved sister Dorothy—the two were never again to live apart—and their move in 1797 to Alfoxden House, near Bristol. There Wordsworth became friends with a fellow poet, Samuel Taylor Coleridge, and they formed a partnership that would change both poets' lives and alter the course of English poetry.

Their partnership was rooted in one marvelous year (1797–98) in which they "together wantoned in wild Poesy."

Stimulated by Coleridge and under the healing influences of nature and his sister, Wordsworth began to compose the short lyrical and dramatic poems for which he is best remembered. Some of these were affectionate tributes to Dorothy, some were tributes to daffodils, birds, and other elements of "Nature's holy plan," and some were portraits of simple rural people intended to illustrate basic truths of human nature. Many of these short poems were written to a daringly original program formulated jointly by Wordsworth and Coleridge, and aimed at breaking the decorum of Neoclassical verse. These poems appeared in 1798 in a slim, anonymously authored volume entitled *Lyrical Ballads*, which opened with Coleridge's long poem *The Rime of the Ancient Mariner* and closed with Wordsworth's *Tintern Abbey*. All but three of the intervening poems were Wordsworth's. The manifesto and the accompanying poems thus set forth a new style, a new vocabulary, and new subjects for poetry, all of them foreshadowing 20th-century developments.

About 1798 Wordsworth began writing the autobiographical poem that would absorb him intermittently for the next 40 years, and which was eventually published in 1850 under the title *The Prelude, or, Growth of a Poet's Mind*. *The Prelude* extends the quiet autobiographical mode of reminiscence that Wordsworth had begun in *Tintern Abbey* and traces the poet's life from his school days through his university life and his visits to France, up to 1799.

In the company of Dorothy, Wordsworth spent the winter of 1798–99 in Germany. Upon his return to England—where he took possession of Dove Cottage, at Grasmere, Westmorland, where he was to reside for eight of his most productive years—Wordsworth incorporated several new poems in the second edition of *Lyrical Ballads*

(1800), notably two tragic pastorals of country life, *The Brothers* and *Michael.* These poems, together with the brilliant lyrics that were assembled in Wordsworth's second verse collection, *Poems, in Two Volumes* (1807), help to make up what is now recognized as his great decade, stretching from his meeting with Coleridge in 1797 until 1808.

In his middle period Wordsworth invested a good deal of his creative energy in odes, the best known of which is *On the Power of Sound.* He also produced a large number of sonnets, most of them strung together in sequences.

In 1808 Wordsworth and his family moved from Dove Cottage to larger quarters in Grasmere, and five years later they settled at Rydal Mount, near Ambleside, where Wordsworth spent the remainder of his life. In 1813 he accepted the post of distributor of stamps for the county of Westmorland.

Through all these years Wordsworth was assailed by vicious and tireless critical attacks by contemptuous reviewers. But by the mid-1830s his reputation had been established with both critics and the reading public. Wordsworth succeeded his friend Robert Southey as Britain's poet laureate in 1843 and held that post until his own death in 1850. Wordsworth's last years were given over partly to "tinkering" his poems, as the family called his compulsive and persistent habit of revising his earlier poems through edition after edition. *The Prelude*, for instance, went through four distinct manuscript versions (1798–99, 1805–06, 1818–20, and 1832–39) and was published only after the poet's death in 1850. Most readers find the earliest versions of *The Prelude* and other heavily revised poems to be the best, but flashes of brilliance can appear in revisions added when the poet was in his seventies.

SIR WALTER SCOTT, 1ST BARONET

(b. Aug. 15, 1771, Edinburgh, Scot.—d. Sept. 21, 1832, Abbotsford, Roxburgh)

The Scottish novelist, poet, historian, and biographer Sir Walter Scott is often considered both the inventor and the greatest practitioner of the historical novel.

In 1786 Scott was apprenticed to his father as writer to the signet, a Scots equivalent of the English solicitor (attorney). His study and practice of law were somewhat desultory, for his immense youthful energy was diverted into social activities and miscellaneous readings in Italian, Spanish, French, German, and Latin. In the mid-1790s Scott became interested in German Romanticism, Gothic novels, and Scottish border ballads. His first published work, *The Chase, and William and Helen* (1796), was a translation of two ballads by the German Romantic balladeer G.A. Bürger. Scott's interest in border ballads finally bore fruit in his collection of them entitled *Minstrelsy of the Scottish Border*, 3 vol. (1802–03). His attempts to "restore" the orally corrupted versions back to their original compositions sometimes resulted in powerful poems that show a sophisticated Romantic flavor. The work made Scott's name known to a wide public, and he followed up his first success with a full-length narrative poem, *The Lay of the Last Minstrel* (1805), which ran into many editions. The poem's clear and vigorous storytelling, Scottish regionalist elements, honest pathos, and vivid evocations of landscape were repeated in further poetic romances, including *The Lady of the Lake* (1810), which was the most successful of these pieces.

Scott led a highly active literary and social life during these years, but his finances now took the first of several disastrous turns. He had become a partner in a printing

Sir Walter Scott (1771–1832) is best known for his historical novels.

(and later publishing) firm owned by James Ballantyne and his irresponsible brother John. By 1813 this firm was hovering on the brink of financial disaster, and although Scott saved the company from bankruptcy, from that time onward everything he wrote was done partly in order to make money and pay off the lasting debts he had incurred. Another ruinous expenditure was the country house he was having built at Abbotsford, which he stocked with enormous quantities of antiquarian objects.

By 1813 Scott had begun to tire of narrative poetry. That year he rediscovered the unfinished manuscript of a novel he had started in 1805, and in the early summer of 1814 he wrote with extraordinary speed almost the whole of his novel, which he titled *Waverley*. A story of the Jacobite rebellion of 1745, it reinterpreted and presented with living force the manners and loyalties of a vanished Scottish Highland society. The book was published anonymously, as were all of the many novels he wrote down to 1827.

In *Waverley* and succeeding novels Scott's particular literary gifts—as a born storyteller and a master of dialogue who possessed a flair for picturesque incidents and a rich, ornate, seemingly effortless literary style—could be utilized to their fullest extent. These immensely popular novels, now known as the *Waverley* novels, include *Guy Mannering* (1815) and *The Antiquary* (1816), which with *Waverley* completed a sort of trilogy covering the period from the 1740s to just after 1800. The first of four series of novels published under the title *Tales of My Landlord* was composed of *The Black Dwarf* and the masterpiece *Old Mortality* (1816). These were followed by the masterpieces *Rob Roy* (1817) and *The Heart of Midlothian* (1818), and then by *The Bride of Lammermoor* and *A Legend of Montrose* (both 1819). He then turned to themes from English history and elsewhere and wrote *Ivanhoe* (1819), a novel set in 12th-century England and one that remains his most popular book. Two more masterpieces were *Kenilworth* (1821), set in Elizabethan England, and the highly successful *Quentin Durward* (1823), set in 15th-century France. The best of his later novels are *Redgauntlet* (1824) and *The Talisman* (1825), the latter being set in Palestine during the Crusades.

Scott's immense earnings in those years contributed to his financial downfall. Eager to own an estate and to act the part of a bountiful laird, he anticipated his income and involved himself in exceedingly complicated and ultimately disastrous financial agreements with his publisher, Archibald Constable, and his agents, the Ballantynes. When Constable was unable to meet his liabilities and went bankrupt, he dragged down the Ballantynes and Scott in his wake because their financial interests were inextricably intermingled. Scott assumed personal responsibility for both his and the Ballantynes' liabilities and thus dedicated himself for the rest of his life to paying off debts amounting to about £120,000.

The result was reckless haste in the production of all his later books and compulsive work whose strain shortened his life, though his rapidity and ease of writing remained largely unimpaired, as did his popularity. Scott's creditors were not hard with him during this period, however, and he was generally revered as the grand old man of English letters. In 1827 Scott's authorship of the *Waverley* novels was finally made public. In 1831 his health deteriorated sharply, and he tried a continental tour with a long stay at Naples to aid recovery. He was taken home and died in 1832.

SAMUEL TAYLOR COLERIDGE

(b. Oct. 21, 1772, Ottery St. Mary, Devonshire, Eng.—d. July 25, 1834, Highgate, near London)

Samuel Taylor Coleridge was an English lyrical poet, critic, and philosopher. His *Lyrical Ballads*, written with William Wordsworth, heralded the English Romantic movement, and his *Biographia Literaria* (1817) is the most significant work of general literary criticism produced in the English Romantic period.

In 1791 Coleridge entered Jesus College, Cambridge. In his third year there, oppressed by financial difficulties, he went to London and enlisted as a dragoon under the assumed name of Silas Tomkyn Comberbache. Despite his unfitness for the life, he remained until discovered by his friends; he was then bought out by his brothers and restored to Cambridge. A chance meeting with the poet Robert Southey led to a close association between the two men and a plan, eventually aborted, to set up a utopian community in Pennsylvania.

Despite these difficulties, Coleridge's intellect flowered in an extraordinary manner during this period, as he embarked on an investigation of the nature of the human mind, joined by William Wordsworth, with whom he had become acquainted in 1795. Together they entered upon one of the most influential creative periods of English literature. Coleridge was developing a new, informal mode of poetry in which he could use a conversational tone and rhythm to give unity to a poem, best exemplified by *Frost at Midnight*.

That poem was an element of Coleridge's exploration of the possibility that all religions and mythical traditions, with their general agreement on the unity of God and the immortality of the soul, sprang from a universal life consciousness, which was expressed particularly through the phenomena of human genius. While these speculations were at their most intense, Coleridge, according to his own account, composed under the influence of laudanum the mysterious poetic fragment known as *Kubla Khan*. The exotic imagery and rhythmic chant of this poem have led many critics to conclude that it should be read as a "meaningless reverie," but it is, like *Frost at Midnight*, a complex poem about the nature of human genius.

Coleridge was enabled to explore similar themes in *The Rime of the Ancient Mariner*, composed during the autumn and winter of 1797–98. For this, his most famous poem, he drew upon the ballad form. The main narrative, infused with supernatural elements, tells how a sailor who has committed a crime against the life principle by slaying an albatross suffers from torments, physical and mental, in which the nature of his crime is made known to him. The placing of it at the beginning of *Lyrical Ballads* (1798) was evidently intended by Coleridge and Wordsworth to provide a context for the sense of wonder in common life that marks many of Wordsworth's contributions.

The decade following the publication of *Lyrical Ballads* were troubled years for Coleridge. He split with Wordsworth, and opium retained its powerful hold on him; the writings that survive from this period are redolent of unhappiness, with self-dramatization veering toward self-pity. In spite of this, however, there also appear signs of a slow revival. A course of lectures on Shakespeare he delivered during the winter of 1811–12 attracted a large audience. Coleridge's play *Osorio*, written many years before, was also produced at Drury Lane with the title *Remorse* in January 1813.

After Coleridge read the 17th-century archbishop Robert Leighton's commentary on the First Letter of

Peter, Christianity, hitherto one point of reference for Coleridge, became his "official" creed. By aligning himself with the Anglican church of the 17th century at its best, he hoped to find a firm point of reference that would both keep him in communication with orthodox Christians of his time (thus giving him the social approval he always needed, even if only from a small group of friends) and enable him to pursue his former intellectual explorations in the hope of reaching a Christian synthesis that might help to revitalize the English church both intellectually and emotionally.

One effect was a sense of liberation and an ability to produce large works again. He drew together a collection of his poems (published in 1817 as *Sibylline Leaves*) and wrote *Biographia Literaria* (1817), a rambling and discursive but highly influential work in which he outlined the evolution of his thought and developed an extended critique of Wordsworth's poems. For the general reader *Biographia Literaria* is a misleading volume, since it moves bewilderingly between autobiography, abstruse philosophical discussion, and literary criticism. But over the whole work hovers Coleridge's veneration for the power of imagination.

His final decades were more settled years. His election as a fellow of the Royal Society of Literature in 1824 brought him an annuity and a sense of recognition. In 1830 he joined the controversy that had arisen around the issue of Catholic Emancipation by writing his last prose work, *On the Constitution of the Church and State*. The third edition of Coleridge's *Poetical Works* appeared in time for him to see it before his final illness and death in 1834.

Coleridge's achievement has been given more widely varying assessments than that of any other English literary artist, though there is broad agreement that his enormous potential was never fully realized in his works.

JANE AUSTEN

(b. Dec. 16, 1775, Steventon, Hampshire, Eng.—d. July 18, 1817, Winchester, Hampshire)

Jane Austen is the English writer who first gave the novel its distinctly modern character through her treatment of ordinary people in everyday life. Austen also created the comedy of manners of middle-class life in the England of her time in her novels.

Austen was born in the Hampshire village of Steventon, where her father, the Reverend George Austen, was rector. She was the seventh child in a family of eight. Her closest companion throughout her life was her elder sister, Cassandra, who also remained unmarried. Their father was a scholar who encouraged the love of learning in his children. His wife, Cassandra, was a woman of ready wit, famed for her impromptu verses and stories. The great family amusement was acting.

Jane Austen's lively and affectionate family circle provided a stimulating context for her writing. Moreover, her experience was carried far beyond Steventon rectory by an extensive network of relationships by blood and friendship. It was this world—of the minor landed gentry and the country clergy, in the village, the neighborhood, and the country town, with occasional visits to Bath and to London—that she was to use in the settings, characters, and subject matter of her novels.

Her earliest-known writings date from about 1787, and between then and 1793 she wrote a large body of material that has survived in three manuscript notebooks. These contain plays, verses, short novels, and other prose and show Austen engaged in the parody of existing literary forms, notably sentimental fiction. Her passage to a more serious view of life from the exuberant high spirits and

Jane Austen penned plays, poems, and short stories as a young lady and continued storytelling until her final illness made it impossible. Austen's productivity is rivaled only by her longevity. She remains a beloved author to this day.

extravagances of her earliest writings is evident in *Lady Susan*, a short novel-in-letters written about 1793–94 (and not published until 1871).

In 1802 it seems likely that Austen agreed to marry Harris Bigg-Wither, the 21-year-old heir of a Hampshire family, but the next morning changed her mind. There are also a number of mutually contradictory stories connecting her with someone with whom she fell in love but who died very soon after. Since Austen's novels are so deeply concerned with love and marriage, there is some point in attempting to establish the facts of these relationships. Unfortunately, the evidence is unsatisfactory and incomplete.

The earliest of her novels, *Sense and Sensibility*, was begun about 1795. Between October 1796 and August 1797 Austen completed the first version of *Pride and Prejudice*. In 1797 her father wrote to offer it to a London publisher for publication, but the offer was declined. *Northanger Abbey*, the last of the early novels, was written about 1798 or 1799, probably under the title "Susan." In 1803 the manuscript of "Susan" was sold to the publisher Richard Crosby for £10. He took it for immediate publication, but, although it was advertised, unaccountably it never appeared during her lifetime.

After years of unsettled lodgings, as a result of the family's move to Bath, Austen's brother Edward was able in 1809 to provide his mother and sisters with a large cottage in the village of Chawton, within his Hampshire estate, not far from Steventon. The prospect of settling at Chawton had already given Austen a renewed sense of purpose, and she began to prepare *Sense and Sensibility* and *Pride and Prejudice* for publication. Two years later Thomas Egerton agreed to publish *Sense and Sensibility*, which came out, anonymously, in November 1811. Both of the leading reviews, the *Critical Review* and the *Quarterly Review*, welcomed its blend of instruction and amusement. Meanwhile, in 1811 Austen had begun the most serious of her novels, *Mansfield Park*, which was finished in 1813 and published in 1814. *Pride and Prejudice* seems to have been the fashionable novel of its season. Between January 1814 and March 1815 she wrote *Emma*, which appeared in December 1815; of her novels it is the most consistently comic in tone. *Persuasion* (written August 1815–August 1816) was published posthumously, with *Northanger Abbey*, in December 1817.

The years after 1811 seem to have been the most rewarding of her life. She had the satisfaction of seeing her work in print and well reviewed and of knowing that the novels were widely read. They were so much enjoyed by the Prince Regent (later George IV) that he had a set in each of his residences; and *Emma*, at a discreet royal command, was "respectfully dedicated" to him.

For the last 18 months of her life, she was busy writing. In January 1817 she began *Sanditon*, a robust and self-mocking satire on health resorts and invalidism. This novel remained unfinished owing to Austen's declining health. In April she made her will, and in May she was taken to Winchester to be under the care of an expert surgeon. She died on July 18, and six days later she was buried in Winchester Cathedral. Her authorship was announced to the world at large by her brother Henry, who supervised the publication of *Northanger Abbey* and *Persuasion*. There was no recognition at the time that regency England had lost its keenest observer and sharpest analyst.

GEORGE GORDON BYRON, 6TH BARON BYRON

(b. Jan. 22, 1788, London, Eng.—d. April 19, 1824, Missolonghi, Greece)

Lord Byron was a British Romantic poet and satirist whose poetry and personality captured the imagination of Europe.

In 1805 Byron entered Trinity College, Cambridge, where he piled up debts at an alarming rate and indulged in the conventional vices of undergraduates there. His first published volume of poetry, *Hours of Idleness*, appeared in 1807. A sarcastic critique of the book in *The Edinburgh Review* provoked his retaliation in 1809 with a couplet satire, *English Bards and Scotch Reviewers*, in which he attacked the contemporary literary scene. This work gained him his first recognition.

In 1809 Byron took his seat in the House of Lords, and then embarked on a grand tour of Europe. In Greece Byron began *Childe Harolde's Pilgrimage*, which he continued in Athens. In March 1810 he sailed for Constantinople (now Istanbul, Turkey), visited the site of Troy, and swam the Hellespont (present-day Dardanelles) in imitation of Leander. In March 1812, the first two cantos of *Childe Harold's Pilgrimage* were published by John Murray, and Byron "woke to find himself famous." The poem describes the travels and reflections of a young man who, disillusioned with a life of pleasure and revelry, looks for distraction in foreign lands. Besides furnishing a travelogue of Byron's own wanderings through the Mediterranean, the first two cantos express the melancholy and disillusionment felt by a generation weary of the wars of the post-Revolutionary and Napoleonic eras.

During the summer of 1813, Byron apparently entered into intimate relations with his half sister Augusta, now married to Colonel George Leigh. He then carried on a flirtation with Lady Frances Webster as a diversion from this dangerous liaison. The agitations of these two love affairs and the sense of mingled guilt and exultation they aroused in Byron are reflected in a series of gloomy and remorseful verse tales he wrote at this time, including *The Corsair* (1814), which sold 10,000 copies on the day of publication.

Seeking to escape his love affairs in marriage, Byron proposed in September 1814 to Anne Isabella (Annabella) Milbanke. The marriage took place in January 1815, and Lady Byron gave birth to a daughter, Augusta Ada, in December 1815. Annabella soon after left Byron to live with her parents, amid swirling rumors centering on his relations with Augusta Leigh and his bisexuality. Wounded by the general moral indignation directed at him, Byron went abroad in April 1816, never to return to England.

Byron sailed up the Rhine River into Switzerland and settled at Geneva, near Percy Bysshe Shelley and Mary Godwin, who had eloped, and Godwin's stepdaughter by a second marriage, Claire Clairmont, with whom Byron had begun an affair in England. In Geneva he wrote the third canto of *Childe Harold* (1816), which, perhaps predictably, follows Harold from Belgium up the Rhine River into Switzerland. At the end of the summer the Shelley party left for England, where Claire gave birth to Byron's illegitimate daughter Allegra in January 1817. In May he arrived in Rome, gathering impressions that he recorded in a fourth canto of *Childe Harold* (1818). He also wrote *Beppo*, a poem in ottava rima that satirically contrasts Italian with English manners.

In the light, mock-heroic style of *Beppo* Byron found the form in which he would write his greatest poem, *Don Juan*, a satire in the form of a picaresque verse tale. The first two cantos of *Don Juan* were begun in 1818 and published in July 1819. Byron transformed the legendary libertine Don Juan into an unsophisticated, innocent young man who, though he delightedly succumbs to the beautiful women who pursue him, remains a rational norm against which to view the absurdities and irrationalities of the world.

Shelley and other visitors in 1818 found Byron grown fat, with hair long and turning gray, looking older than his years, and sunk in sexual promiscuity. But a chance meeting with Countess Teresa Gamba Guiccioli, who was only 19 years old and married to a man nearly three times her age, reenergized Byron and changed the course of his life. He won the friendship of her father and brother, Counts Ruggero and Pietro Gamba, respectively, who initiated him into the secret society of the Carbonari and its revolutionary aims to free Italy from Austrian rule. Byron wrote cantos III, IV, and V of *Don Juan* at this time; it and a number of other works were published in 1821.

After collaborating with Shelley and Leigh Hunt on a periodical, Byron's attention wandered. Cantos VI to XVI of *Don Juan* were published in 1823–24 by Hunt's brother John, after Byron quarrelled with his publisher. From April 1823 Byron aided the Greeks in their struggle for independence from the Turks. He made efforts to unite the various Greek factions and took personal command of a brigade of Souliot soldiers, reputedly the bravest of the Greeks. But a serious illness in February 1824 weakened him, and in April he contracted the fever from which he died. Deeply mourned, he became a symbol of disinterested patriotism and a Greek national hero. His body was brought back to England and, refused burial in Westminster Abbey, was placed in the family vault near Newstead.

PERCY BYSSHE SHELLEY

(b. Aug. 4, 1792, Field Place, near Horsham, Sussex, Eng.—d. July 8, 1822, at sea off Livorno, Tuscany [Italy])

Percy Bysshe Shelley was an English Romantic poet whose passionate search for personal love and social justice was gradually channeled from overt actions into poems that rank with the greatest in the English language.

Shelley was the heir to rich estates acquired by his grandfather, Bysshe (pronounced "Bish") Shelley. Between the spring of 1810 and that of 1811, he published two Gothic novels and two volumes of juvenile verse. In the fall of 1810 Shelley entered University College, Oxford; he was expelled the following year. Late in August 1811, Shelley eloped with Harriet Westbrook, the younger daughter of a London tavern owner; by marrying her, he betrayed the acquisitive plans of his grandfather and father, who tried to starve him into submission but only drove the strong-willed youth to rebel against the established order. Early in 1812, Shelley, Harriet, and her older sister Eliza Westbrook went to Dublin, where Shelley circulated pamphlets advocating political rights for Roman Catholics, autonomy for Ireland, and freethinking ideals.

Lack of money finally drove Shelley to moneylenders in London, where in 1813 he issued *Queen Mab*, his first major poem—a nine-canto mixture of blank verse and lyric measures that attacks the evils of the past and present (commerce, war, the eating of meat, the church, monarchy, and marriage) but ends with resplendent hopes for humanity when freed from these vices. In June 1813 Harriet Shelley gave birth to their daughter Ianthe, but a year later Shelley fell in love with Mary Wollstonecraft Godwin, daughter of William Godwin and his first wife, *née* Mary Wollstonecraft. Against Godwin's objections, Shelley and Mary Godwin eloped to France on July 27,

1814. Following travels through France, Switzerland, and Germany, they returned to London, where they were shunned by the Godwins and most other friends.

By mid-May 1816, Shelley, Mary, and Mary's stepsister Claire Clairmont hurried to Geneva to intercept Lord Byron, with whom Claire had begun an affair. During this memorable summer, Shelley composed the poems "Hymn to Intellectual Beauty" and "Mont Blanc," and Mary began her novel *Frankenstein*, the novel for which she would become best known. Shelley's party returned to England in September, settling in Bath. Late in the year, Harriet Shelley drowned herself in London, and on December 30, 1816, Shelley and Mary were married with the Godwins' blessing.

In March 1817 the Shelleys settled near Peacock at Marlow, where Shelley wrote his twelve-canto romance-epic *Laon and Cythna; or, The Revolution of the Golden City* and Mary Shelley finished *Frankenstein*. They compiled *History of a Six Weeks' Tour* jointly from the letters and journals of their trips to Switzerland. In November, *Laon and Cythna* was suppressed by its printer and publisher, who feared that Shelley's idealized tale of a peaceful national revolution, bloodily suppressed by a league of king and priests, violated the laws against blasphemous libel. After revisions, it was reissued in 1818 as *The Revolt of Islam*. Because Shelley's health suffered from the climate and his financial obligations outran his resources, the Shelleys and Claire Clairmont went to Italy, where Byron was residing.

Thus far, Shelley's literary career had been politically oriented. But in Italy, far from the daily irritations of British politics, Shelley deepened his understanding of art and literature and, unable to reshape the world to conform to his vision, he concentrated on embodying his ideals within his poems.

In early 1818–19 Shelley wrote *Prometheus Unbound* and outlined *The Cenci*, a tragedy on the Elizabethan model based on a case of incestuous rape and patricide in sixteenth-century Rome. He completed this drama during the summer of 1819. Memorable characters, classic five-act structure, powerful and evocative language, and moral ambiguities still make *The Cenci* theatrically effective. Even so, it is a less notable achievement than *Prometheus Unbound: A Lyrical Drama*, the keystone of Shelley's poetic achievement, which Shelley completed at Florence in the autumn of 1819. Both plays appeared about 1820.

After moving to Pisa in 1820, Shelley was stung by hostile reviews into expressing his hopes more guardedly. In 1821, however, he reasserted his uncompromising idealism. *Epipsychidion* (in couplets) mythologizes his infatuation with Teresa ("Emilia") Viviani, a convent-bound young admirer, into a Dantesque fable of how human desire can be fulfilled through art. His essay *A Defence of Poetry* (published 1840) eloquently declares that the poet creates humane values and imagines the forms that shape the social order: thus each mind recreates its own private universe, and "Poets are the unacknowledged legislators of the World."

After the Shelleys moved to Lerici in 1822, Percy Shelley began *The Triumph of Life*, a dark fragment on which he was at work until he sailed to Leghorn to welcome his friend Leigh Hunt, who had arrived to edit a periodical called *The Liberal*. Shelley drowned on July 8, 1822, when his boat sank during the stormy return voyage to Lerici.

After her husband's death, Mary Shelley returned to England and devoted herself to publicizing Shelley's writings and educating their only surviving child, Percy Florence Shelley. She published her late husband's

Posthumous Poems (1824) and also edited his *Poetical Works* (1839), with long and invaluable notes, and his prose works. Her *Journal* is a rich source of Shelley biography, and her letters are an indispensable adjunct. By 1840 she had disseminated his fame and most of his writings.

JOHN KEATS

(b. Oct. 31, 1795, London, Eng.—d. Feb. 23, 1821, Rome, Papal States [Italy])

John Keats was an English Romantic lyric poet who devoted his short life to the perfection of a poetry marked by vivid imagery, great sensuous appeal, and an attempt to express a philosophy through classical legend.

The son of a livery-stable manager, Keats received relatively little formal education. He was apprenticed to a surgeon in 1811, but he broke off his apprenticeship in 1814 and went to live in London, where he worked as a dresser, or junior house surgeon, at Guy's and St. Thomas' hospitals. After 1817 he devoted himself entirely to poetry.

His first mature poem is the sonnet *On First Looking Into Chapman's Homer* (1816), which was inspired by his excited reading of George Chapman's classic 17th-century translation of the *Iliad* and the *Odyssey*. Keats's first book, *Poems*, was published in March 1817. The volume is remarkable only for some delicate natural observation and some obvious Spenserian influences.

In 1817 Keats began work on *Endymion*, his first long poem, which appeared in 1818. This work is divided into four 1,000-line sections, and its verse is composed in loose rhymed couplets. The poem narrates a version of the Greek legend of the moon goddess Diana's (or Cynthia's) love for Endymion, a mortal shepherd, but Keats put the emphasis on Endymion's love for Diana rather than on

John Keats (1795–1821) left a legacy of well-loved lyric poems.

hers for him and thus transformed the tale to express the widespread Romantic theme of the attempt to find in actuality an ideal love that has been glimpsed heretofore only in imaginative longings.

In the summer of 1818 Keats went on a walking tour in the Lake District (of northern England) and Scotland, and his exposure and overexertions on that trip brought on the first symptoms of the tuberculosis of which he was to die. On his return to London a brutal criticism of his early poems appeared in *Blackwood's Magazine*, followed by a similar attack on *Endymion* in the *Quarterly Review*. Contrary to later assertions, Keats met these reviews with a calm assertion of his own talents, and he went on steadily writing poetry. But there were family troubles, and Keats also met Fanny Brawne, a near neighbor in Hampstead, with whom he soon fell hopelessly and tragically in love. The relation with Brawne had a decisive effect on Keats's development.

It was during the year 1819 that all his greatest poetry was written—*Lamia*, *The Eve of St. Agnes*, the great odes (*On Indolence*, *On a Grecian Urn*, *To Psyche*, *To a Nightingale*, *On Melancholy*, and *To Autumn*), and the two versions of *Hyperion*. This poetry was composed under the strain of illness and his growing love for Brawne; and it is an astonishing body of work, marked by careful and considered development, technical, emotional, and intellectual. *The Eve of St. Agnes* may be considered the perfect culmination of Keats's earlier poetic style. Written in the first flush of his meeting with Brawne, it conveys an atmosphere of passion and excitement in its description of the elopement of a pair of youthful lovers.

The odes are Keats's most distinctive poetic achievement. In the *Ode to a Nightingale* a visionary happiness in communing with the nightingale and its song is contrasted with the dead weight of human grief and sickness, and the transience of youth and beauty—strongly brought home to Keats in recent months by the death of one of his brothers. This theme is taken up more distinctly in the *Ode on a Grecian Urn*. The figures of the lovers depicted on the Greek urn become for him the symbol of an enduring but unconsummated passion that subtly belies the poem's celebrated conclusion, "Beauty is truth, truth beauty,—that is all ye know on earth, and all ye need to know."

Keats's fragmentary poetic epic, *Hyperion*, exists in two versions, the second being a revision of the first with the addition of a long prologue in a new style, which makes it into a different poem. *Hyperion* was begun in the autumn of 1818, and all that there is of the first version was finished by April 1819. These two versions cover the period of Keats's most intense experience, both poetical and personal. The poem is his last attempt, in the face of increasing illness and frustrated love, to come to terms with the conflict between absolute value and mortal decay that appears in other forms in his earlier poetry.

The poems *Isabella*, *Lamia*, *The Eve of St. Agnes*, and *Hyperion* and the odes were all published in the famous 1820 volume, the one that gives the true measure of his powers. He had been increasingly ill throughout 1819, and by the beginning of 1820 the evidence of tuberculosis was clear. He realized that it was his death warrant, and from that time sustained work became impossible. Keats sailed for Italy in September 1820; when he reached Rome, he had a relapse and died there.

ALEKSANDR PUSHKIN

(b. May 26 [June 6, New Style], 1799, Moscow, Russia—d. Jan. 29 [Feb. 10], 1837, St. Petersburg)

The Russian poet, novelist, dramatist, and short-story writer Aleksandr Sergeyevich Pushkin has often been considered his country's greatest poet and the founder of modern Russian literature.

In 1817 Pushkin accepted a post in the foreign office at St. Petersburg, where he was elected to Arzamás, an exclusive literary circle founded by his uncle's friends. In his political verses and epigrams, widely circulated in manuscript, he made himself the spokesman for the ideas and aspirations of those who were to take part in the Decembrist rising of 1825, the unsuccessful culmination of a Russian revolutionary movement in its earliest stage.

For these political poems, Pushkin was banished from St. Petersburg in May 1820 to a remote southern province. Sent first to Yekaterinoslav (now Dnipropetrovsk, Ukraine), he was there taken ill. While convalescing, he traveled in the northern Caucasus and later to the Crimea. The impressions he gained provided material for his "southern cycle" of romantic narrative poems, published 1820–23. Although this cycle of poems confirmed the reputation of the author of *Ruslan i Lyudmila* (1820; *Ruslan and Ludmila*), his first major work, and Pushkin was hailed as the leading Russian poet of the day, he himself was not satisfied with it. In May 1823 he started work on his central masterpiece, the novel in verse *Yevgeny Onegin* (1833), on which he continued to work intermittently until 1831. *Yevgeny Onegin* unfolds a panoramic picture of Russian life. The characters it depicts and immortalizes—Onegin, the disenchanted skeptic; Lensky, the romantic, freedom-loving poet; and Tatyana, the heroine, a profoundly affectionate study of

Russian womanhood—are typically Russian and are shown in relationship to the social and environmental forces by which they are molded.

Remarks in letters intercepted by police resulted in Pushkin being exiled to his mother's estate of Mikhaylovskoye, near Pskov, at the other end of Russia. Although the two years at Mikhaylovskoye were unhappy for Pushkin, they were to prove one of his most productive periods. Alone and isolated, he embarked on a close study of Russian history; he came to know the peasants on the estate and interested himself in noting folktales and songs. During this period the specifically Russian features of his poetry became steadily more marked. He wrote the provincial chapters of *Yevgeny Onegin* as well as one of his major works, the historical tragedy *Boris Godunov* (1831). Written just before the Decembrist uprising, *Boris Godunov* treats the burning question of the relations between the ruling classes, headed by the tsar, and the masses; it is the moral and political significance of the latter, "the judgment of the people," that Pushkin emphasizes. Pushkin's ability to create psychological and dramatic unity, despite the episodic construction, and to heighten the dramatic tension by economy of language, detail, and characterization make this outstanding play a revolutionary event in the history of Russian drama.

After the suppression of the Decembrist uprising, the new tsar Nicholas I, aware of Pushkin's immense popularity and knowing that he had taken no part in the Decembrist "conspiracy," allowed him to return to Moscow in the autumn of 1826. During a long conversation between them, the tsar met the poet's complaints about censorship with a promise that in the future he himself would be Pushkin's censor and told him of his plans to introduce several pressing reforms from above and, in particular, to prepare the way for liberation of the serfs.

Pushkin saw, however, that without the support of the people, the struggle against autocracy was doomed. He considered that the only possible way of achieving essential reforms was from above, "on the tsar's initiative." This is the reason for his persistent interest in the age of reforms at the beginning of the 18th century and in the figure of Peter the Great, the "tsar-educator," whose example he held up to the present tsar in, among other works, the poem *Medny vsadnik* (1837; *The Bronze Horseman*). The poem describes how the "little hero," Yevgeny, driven mad by the drowning of his sweetheart, wanders through the streets. Seeing the bronze statue of Peter I seated on a rearing horse and realizing that the tsar, seen triumphing over the waves, is the cause of his grief, Yevgeny threatens him. In a climax of growing horror, he is pursued through the streets by the "Bronze Horseman." The poem's descriptive and emotional powers give it an unforgettable impact and make it one of the greatest in Russian literature.

It was during this period that Pushkin's genius came to its fullest flowering, despite his being surveilled by the police and struggling against the tsar's censorship. His art acquired new dimensions, and almost every one of the many works written between 1829 and 1836 opened a new chapter in the history of Russian literature.

In 1831, Pushkin married Natalya Nikolayevna Goncharova and settled in St. Petersburg. Once more he took up government service. The social life at court, which he was now obliged to lead and which his wife enjoyed, was ill-suited to creative work, but he stubbornly continued to write. Alongside the theme of Peter the Great, the motif of a popular peasant rising acquired growing importance in his work, as is shown in particular by the most important of his prose works, the historical novel of the Pugachov Rebellion, *Kapitanskaya dochka* (1836; *The Captain's Daughter*). In court circles he was regarded with mounting suspicion and resentment, however, and his repeated petitions to be allowed to retire to the country and devote himself entirely to literature were all rejected. In 1837, Pushkin was mortally wounded defending his wife's honor in a duel forced on him by influential enemies.

VICTOR HUGO

(b. Feb. 26, 1802, Besançon, France—d. May 22, 1885, Paris)

Victor Hugo was a poet, novelist, and dramatist, and the most important of the French Romantic writers. Though regarded in France as one of that country's greatest poets, he is better known abroad for such novels as *Notre-Dame de Paris* (1831) and *Les Misérables* (1862).

The son of a general, Hugo was an accomplished poet before age 20. With his verse drama *Cromwell* (1827), though immensely long and almost impossible to stage, he emerged as an important figure in Romanticism. The production of his verse tragedy *Hernani*, on February 25, 1830, gained victory for the young Romantics over the Classicists in what came to be known as the battle of *Hernani*. In this play Hugo extolled the Romantic hero in the form of a noble outlaw at war with society, dedicated to a passionate love and driven on by inexorable fate.

Hugo gained wider fame in 1831 with his historical novel *Notre-Dame de Paris* (Eng. trans. *The Hunchback of Notre-Dame*), an evocation of life in medieval Paris during the reign of Louis XI. The novel condemns a society that, in the persons of Frollo the archdeacon and Phoebus the soldier, heaps misery on the hunchback Quasimodo and the gypsy girl Esmeralda.

So intense was Hugo's creative activity in the 1830s and 1840s that he also continued to pour out plays. There were two motives for this: first, he needed a platform for his political and social ideas, and, second, he wished to write parts for a young and beautiful actress, Juliette Drouet, with whom he had begun a liaison in 1833. The first of these plays was another verse drama, *Le Roi s'amuse* (1832; Eng. trans. *The King's Fool*).

Hugo's literary achievement was recognized in 1841 by his election, after three unsuccessful attempts, to the French Academy and by his nomination in 1845 to the Chamber of Peers. From this time he almost ceased to publish, partly because of the demands of society and political life but also as a result of personal loss: his daughter Léopoldine, recently married, was accidentally drowned with her husband in September 1843. He found relief above all in working on a new novel, which became *Les Misérables*, published in 1862 after work on it had been set aside for a time and then resumed.

Hugo's republican views drove him into exile—at first enforced, then voluntary—between 1851 and 1870. During this exile he produced the most extensive part of all his writings and the most original, including *Les Châtiments* (1853; "The Punishments"), among the most powerful satirical poems in the French language, and *Les Contemplations* (1856), which contains the purest of his poetry.

Hugo then returned to prose and took up his abandoned novel, *Les Misérables*. Its extraordinary success with readers of every type when it was published in 1862 brought him instant popularity in his own country, and its speedy translation into many languages won him fame abroad. The novel's name means "the wretched," or "the outcasts," but English translations generally carry the French title. The story centers on the convict Jean Valjean,

Victor Hugo (1802–1885) is considered the most important writer of the French Romantic movement.

a victim of society who has been imprisoned for 19 years for stealing a loaf of bread. *Les Misérables* is a vast panorama of Parisian society and its underworld, and it contains many famous episodes and passages, among them a chapter on the Battle of Waterloo and the description of Jean Valjean's rescue of his daughter's husband by means of a flight through the sewers of Paris.

Hugo's enormous output is unique in French literature; it is said that he wrote each morning 100 lines of verse or 20 pages of prose. "The most powerful mind of the Romantic movement," as he was described in 1830, laureate and peer of France in 1845, he went on to assume the role of an outlawed sage who, with the easy consciousness of authority, put down his insights and prophetic visions in prose and verse, becoming at last the genial grandfather of popular literary portraiture and the national poet who gave his name to a street in every town in France.

NATHANIEL HAWTHORNE

(b. July 4, 1804, Salem, Mass., U.S.—d. May 19, 1864, Plymouth, N.H.)

The American novelist and short-story writer Nathaniel Hawthorne was a master of the allegorical and symbolic tale. One of the greatest fiction writers in American literature, he is best known for *The Scarlet Letter* (1850) and *The House of the Seven Gables* (1851).

Hawthorne did not distinguish himself as a young man. Instead, he spent nearly a dozen years reading and trying to master the art of writing fiction. His first novel, *Fanshawe*, which he published at his own expense in 1825, upon graduation from Bowdoin College, he considered a failure. Hawthorne, however, soon found his own voice, style, and subjects, and by 1830 he had published such impressive and distinctive stories as "The

Hollow of the Three Hills" and "An Old Woman's Tale." By 1832, "My Kinsman, Major Molineux" and "Roger Malvin's Burial," two of his greatest tales—and among the finest in the language—had appeared. "Young Goodman Brown," perhaps the greatest tale of witchcraft ever written, appeared in 1835.

His first signed book, *Twice-Told Tales*, was published in 1837. By 1842, Hawthorne's writing had brought him a sufficient income to allow him to marry Sophia Peabody; the couple rented the Old Manse in Concord and began a happy period that Hawthorne would later record in his essay "The Old Manse."

The presence of some of the leading social thinkers and philosophers of his day, such as Ralph Waldo Emerson, Henry Thoreau, and Bronson Alcott, in Concord made the village the center of the philosophy of Transcendentalism. Hawthorne welcomed the companionship of his Transcendentalist neighbors, but he had little to say to them. His new short-story collection, *Mosses from an Old Manse*, appeared in 1846, a year after he had moved to Salem, where he had been appointed to the position of surveyor of the Custom House.

In a few months of concentrated effort in 1848, he produced his masterpiece, *The Scarlet Letter*. (The bitterness he felt over his dismissal from the Salem Custom House in 1848, which had been a political appointment, is apparent in "The Custom House" essay prefixed to the novel.) *The Scarlet Letter* tells the story of two lovers kept apart by the ironies of fate, their own mingled strengths and weaknesses, and the Puritan community's interpretation of moral law, until at last death unites them under a single headstone. The book made Hawthorne famous and was eventually recognized as one of the greatest of American novels.

Determined to leave Salem forever, Hawthorne moved to Lenox, located in the mountain scenery of the Berkshires in western Massachusetts. There he began work on *The House of the Seven Gables* (1851), the story of the Pyncheon family, who for generations had lived under a curse until it was removed at last by love. At Lenox he enjoyed the stimulating friendship of Herman Melville, who lived in nearby Pittsfield. This friendship, although important for the younger writer and his work, was much less so for Hawthorne.

In 1853, when his friend Franklin Pierce assumed the presidency of the United States, Hawthorne was appointed to a consulship in Liverpool, Lancashire. The position was terminated in 1857, and then he spent a year and a half sightseeing in Italy. Determined to produce yet another romance, he finally retreated to a seaside town in England and quickly produced *The Marble Faun*. In writing it, he drew heavily upon the experiences and impressions he had recorded in a notebook kept during his Italian tour to give substance to an allegory of the Fall of Man, a theme that had usually been assumed in his earlier works but that now received direct and philosophic treatment.

Back in Concord in 1860, Hawthorne devoted himself entirely to his writing but was unable to make any progress with his plans for a new novel. The drafts of unfinished works he left are mostly incoherent. Some two years before his death he began to age very suddenly. His hair turned white, his handwriting changed, he suffered frequent nosebleeds, and he took to writing the figure "64" compulsively on scraps of paper. He died in his sleep on a trip with Pierce in search of health.

Hawthorne's high rank among American fiction writers is the result of at least three considerations. First, Hawthorne was a skillful craftsman with an impressive sense of form; second, he had profound moral insight; third, he was a master of allegory and symbolism. Hawthorne was also the master of a literary style that is remarkable for its directness, its clarity, its firmness, and its sureness of idiom. Hawthorne's work initiated the most durable tradition in American fiction, that of the symbolic romance that assumes the universality of guilt and explores the complexities and ambiguities of man's choices. His greatest short stories and *The Scarlet Letter* are marked by a depth of psychological and moral insight seldom equaled by any American writer.

EDGAR ALLAN POE

(b. Jan. 19, 1809, Boston, Mass., U.S.—d. Oct. 7, 1849, Baltimore, Md.)

Edgar Allan Poe was an American short-story writer, poet, critic, and editor who is famous for his cultivation of mystery and the macabre. His tale *The Murders in the Rue Morgue* (1841) initiated the modern detective story, and the atmosphere in his tales of horror is unrivaled in American fiction. His *The Raven* (1845) numbers among the best-known poems in the national literature.

Poe was the son of the English-born actress Elizabeth Arnold Poe and David Poe, Jr., an actor from Baltimore. After his mother died in Richmond, Virginia, in 1811, he was taken into the home of John Allan, a Richmond merchant (presumably his godfather), and of his childless wife. He was later taken to Scotland and England (1815–20), where he was given a classical education that was continued in Richmond. For 11 months in 1826 he attended the University of Virginia, but his gambling losses at the university so incensed his guardian that he refused to let him continue, and Poe returned to Richmond to find his sweetheart, (Sarah) Elmira Royster, engaged. He went to

Edgar Allan Poe (1809–1849) wrote dark and mysterious poems and tales.

Boston, where in 1827 he published a pamphlet of youthful Byronic poems, *Tamerlane, and Other Poems*. Poverty forced him to join the army under the name of Edgar A. Perry, but, on the death of Poe's foster mother, John Allan purchased his release from the army and helped him get an appointment to the U.S. Military Academy at West Point. Before going, Poe published a new volume at Baltimore, *Al Aaraaf, Tamerlane, and Minor Poems* (1829). He successfully sought expulsion from the academy, where he was absent from all drills and classes for a week.

He proceeded to New York City and brought out a volume of *Poems*, containing several masterpieces, some showing the influence of John Keats, Percy Bysshe Shelley, and Samuel Taylor Coleridge. He then returned to Baltimore, where he began to write stories. In 1833 his *MS. Found in a Bottle* won $50 from a Baltimore weekly, and by 1835 he was in Richmond as editor of the *Southern Literary Messenger*. There he made a name as a critical reviewer and married his young cousin Virginia Clemm, who was only 13. Poe seems to have been an affectionate husband and son-in-law.

Poe was dismissed from his job in Richmond, apparently for drinking, and went to New York City. While in New York City in 1838 he published a long prose narrative, *The Narrative of Arthur Gordon Pym*, combining (as so often in his tales) much factual material with the wildest fancies. It is considered one inspiration of Herman Melville's *Moby Dick*. In 1839 he became coeditor of *Burton's Gentleman's Magazine* in Philadelphia. There a contract for a monthly feature stimulated him to write *William Wilson* and *The Fall of the House of Usher*, stories of supernatural horror. The latter contains a study of a neurotic now known to have been an acquaintance of Poe, not Poe himself.

Later in 1839 Poe's *Tales of the Grotesque and Arabesque* appeared (dated 1840). He resigned from *Burton's* about

June 1840 but returned in 1841 to edit its successor, *Graham's Lady's and Gentleman's Magazine*, in which he printed the first detective story, *The Murders in the Rue Morgue*. In 1843 his *The Gold-Bug* won a prize of $100 from the Philadelphia *Dollar Newspaper*, which gave him great publicity. In 1844 he returned to New York, wrote *The Balloon-Hoax* for the *Sun*, and became subeditor of the *New York Mirror* under N. P. Willis, thereafter a lifelong friend. In the *New York Mirror* of January 29, 1845, there appeared, from advance sheets of the *American Review*, his most famous poem, *The Raven*, which gave him national fame at once.

Poe then became editor of the *Broadway Journal*, a short-lived weekly, in which he republished most of his short stories, in 1845. During this last year the now-forgotten poet Frances Sargent Locke Osgood pursued Poe. Virginia did not object, but "Fanny's" indiscreet writings about her literary love caused great scandal. His *The Raven and Other Poems* and a selection of his *Tales* came out in 1845, and in 1846 Poe moved to a cottage at Fordham (now part of New York City), where he wrote *The Literati of New York City* for *Godey's Lady's Book* (May–October 1846). These gossipy sketches on personalities of the day led to a libel suit.

Poe's wife, Virginia, died in January 1847. The following year he went to Providence, Rhode Island, to woo Sarah Helen Whitman, a poet. There was a brief engagement. Poe had close but platonic entanglements with Annie Richmond and with Sarah Anna Lewis, who helped him financially. He composed poetic tributes to all of them. In 1848 he also published the lecture *Eureka*, a transcendental "explanation" of the universe, which has been hailed as a masterpiece by some critics and as nonsense by others. In 1849 he went south, had a wild spree in

Philadelphia, but got safely to Richmond, where he finally became engaged to Elmira Royster, by then the widowed Mrs. Shelton, and spent a happy summer with only one or two relapses. He enjoyed the companionship of childhood friends and an unromantic friendship with a young poet, Susan Archer Talley.

Poe had some forebodings of death when he left Richmond for Baltimore late in September. There he died, although whether from drinking, heart failure, or other causes is still uncertain.

CHARLES DICKENS

(b. Feb. 7, 1812, Portsmouth, Hampshire, Eng.—d. June 9, 1870, Gad's Hill, near Chatham, Kent)

Charles Dickens is generally considered the greatest British novelist of the Victorian period. His origins were middle class, if of a newfound and precarious respectability; one grandfather had been a domestic servant, and the other an embezzler. His father, a clerk in the navy pay office, was well paid, but his extravagance and ineptitude often brought the family to financial embarrassment or disaster. In 1824 the family reached bottom. Charles, the eldest son, had been withdrawn from school and was now sent to do manual work in a factory, and his father went to prison for debt. These shocks deeply affected Charles. Though abhorring this brief descent into the working class, he began to gain that sympathetic knowledge of their life and privations that informed his writings. His schooling, interrupted and unimpressive, ended at 15. He became a clerk in a solicitor's office, then a shorthand reporter in the law courts (thus gaining a knowledge of the legal world often used in the novels), and finally a parliamentary and newspaper reporter.

Much drawn to the theater, Dickens nearly became a professional actor in 1832. In 1833 he began contributing stories and descriptive essays to magazines and newspapers; these attracted attention and were reprinted as *Sketches by "Boz"* (February 1836). The same month, he was invited to provide a comic serial narrative to accompany engravings by a well-known artist; seven weeks later the first installment of *Pickwick Papers* appeared. Within a few months *Pickwick*, his first novel, was the rage and Dickens the most popular author of the day. Resigning from his newspaper job, he undertook to edit a monthly magazine, *Bentley's Miscellany*, in which he serialized his second novel, *Oliver Twist* (1837–39).

Finding serialization congenial and profitable, he repeated the *Pickwick* pattern of 20 monthly parts in *Nicholas Nickleby* (1838–39); then he experimented with shorter weekly installments for *The Old Curiosity Shop* (1840–41) and *Barnaby Rudge* (1841). Exhausted at last, he then took a five-month vacation in America, touring strenuously and receiving quasi-royal honors as a literary celebrity but offending national sensibilities by protesting against the absence of copyright protection.

Novels continued to tumble forth: *Martin Chuzzlewit* (1843–44), *Dombey and Son* (1846–48), *Bleak House* (1852–53), *Little Dorrit* (1855–57). Dickens's popularity was ever-expanding. He had about him "a sort of swell and overflow as of a prodigality of life," an American journalist said, and he cut a dandyish figure in London. His journalistic ambitions at last found a permanent form in *Household Words* (1850–59) and its successor, *All the Year Round* (1859–88), to which he contributed some serialized novels—including *Hard Times* (1854), *A Tale of Two Cities* (1859), and *Great Expectations* (1860–61)—and essays. But in the novels of the 1850s Dickens is politically more

This photo of Charles Dickens (1812–1870) was taken in the 1860s.

despondent, emotionally more tragic. The satire is harsher, the humor less genial and abundant, the "happy endings" more subdued than in the early fiction. This turn was the result partly of political reasons, partly of marital troubles. (The actress Ellen Ternan, 27 years his junior, seems to have become his mistress in the 1860s.)

In April 1858 Dickens began a series of paid public readings, the immediate impulse being to find some energetic distraction from his domestic unhappiness. His readings drew on more permanent elements in him and his art: his remarkable histrionic talents, his love of theatricals and of seeing and delighting an audience, and the eminently performable nature of his fiction. Moreover, he could earn more by reading than by writing, and more certainly; it was easier to force himself to repeat a performance than create a book. His initial repertoire consisted entirely of Christmas books but was soon amplified by episodes from the novels and magazine Christmas stories. A performance usually consisted of two items. Of the 16 eventually performed, the most popular were *The Trial from Pickwick* and *A Christmas Carol* (1834). Comedy predominated, though pathos was important in the repertoire, and horrifics were startlingly introduced in the last reading he devised, *Sikes and Nancy*, with which he petrified his audiences and half killed himself. Intermittently, until shortly before his death, he gave seasons of readings in London and embarked upon hard-working tours through the provinces and (in 1867–68) the United States. Altogether he performed about 471 times.

Tired and ailing though he was in his later years, Dickens remained inventive and adventurous in his final novels. *A Tale of Two Cities* was an experiment, relying less than before on characterization, dialogue, and humor. *Great Expectations*, though not his most ambitious, is his most finely achieved novel. *Our Mutual Friend* (1864–65), a large inclusive novel, offers a critique of monetary and class values. The unfinished *Edwin Drood* (1870) would likely have been his most elaborate treatment of the themes of crime, evil, and psychological abnormality that had recurred throughout his novels. His farewell reading tour was abandoned when, in April 1869, he collapsed. He died suddenly in June 1870 and was buried in Westminster Abbey.

Dickens enjoyed a wider popularity than had any previous author during his lifetime. Much in his work could appeal to simple and sophisticated, to the poor and to the Queen, and technological developments as well as the qualities of his work enabled his fame to spread worldwide very quickly. The most abundantly comic of English authors, he was much more than a great entertainer. The range, compassion, and intelligence of his apprehension of his society and its shortcomings enriched his novels and made him both one of the great forces in 19th-century literature and an influential spokesman of the conscience of his age.

ROBERT BROWNING

(b. May 7, 1812, London, Eng.—d. Dec. 12, 1889, Venice [Italy])

Robert Browning was perhaps the greatest English poet of the Victorian age, noted for his mastery of the dramatic monologue and of psychological portraiture.

Browning received only a slight formal education, although his father gave him a grounding in Greek and Latin. His first published work, *Pauline: A Fragment of a Confession* (1833, anonymous), although formally a dramatic monologue, embodied many of his own adolescent passions and anxieties. Although it received some favorable comment, it was attacked by John Stuart Mill, who condemned the poet's exposure and exploitation of his own emotions and his "intense and morbid self-consciousness." It was perhaps Mill's critique that determined Browning never to confess his own emotions again in his poetry but to write objectively. In 1835 he published *Paracelsus* and in 1840 *Sordello*, both poems dealing with men of great ability striving to reconcile the demands of their own personalities with those of the world. *Paracelsus* was well received, but *Sordello*, which made exacting demands on its reader's knowledge, was almost universally declared incomprehensible.

Encouraged by the actor Charles Macready, Browning devoted his main energies for some years to verse drama, a form that he had already adopted for *Strafford* (1837). Between 1841 and 1846, in a series of pamphlets under the general title of *Bells and Pomegranates*, he published seven more plays in verse, including *Pippa Passes* (1841), *A Blot in the 'Scutcheon* (produced in 1843), and *Luria* (1846). These, and all his earlier works except *Strafford*, were printed at his family's expense. Although Browning enjoyed writing for the stage, he was not successful in the theater, since his strength lay in depicting, as he had himself observed of *Strafford*, "Action in Character, rather than Character in Action."

By 1845 the first phase of Browning's life was near its end. In that year he met Elizabeth Barrett. In her *Poems* (1844) Barrett had included lines praising Browning, who wrote to thank her (January 1845). In May they met and soon discovered their love for each other. Barrett had, however, been for many years an invalid, confined to her room and thought incurable. Her father, moreover, was a dominant and selfish man, jealously fond of his daughter, who in turn had come to depend on his love. When her doctors ordered her to Italy for her health and her father refused to allow her to go, the lovers, who had been corresponding and meeting regularly, were forced to act. They were married secretly in September 1846; a week later they left for Pisa.

Throughout their married life, although they spent holidays in France and England, their home was in Italy, mainly at Florence, where they had a flat in Casa Guidi. Their income was small, although after the birth of their son, Robert, in 1849 Mrs. Browning's cousin John Kenyon made them an allowance of £100 a year, and on his death in 1856 he left them £11,000.

Browning produced comparatively little poetry during his married life. *Men and Women* (1855) was a collection of 51 poems—dramatic lyrics such as *Memorabilia*, *Love Among the Ruins*, and *A Toccata of Galuppi's*; the great monologues such as *Fra Lippo Lippi*, *How It Strikes a Contemporary*, and *Bishop Blougram's Apology*; and a very few poems in which implicitly (*By the Fireside*) or explicitly (*One Word More*) he broke his rule and spoke of himself and of his love for his wife. *Men and Women*, however, had no great sale, and many of the reviews were unfavorable and unhelpful. Disappointed for the first time by the reception of his work, Browning in the following years wrote little, sketching and modeling in clay by day and enjoying the society of his friends at night. At last Mrs. Browning's health, which had been remarkably restored by her life in Italy, began to fail. On June 29, 1861, she died in her husband's arms. In the autumn he returned slowly to London with his young son.

His first task on his return was to prepare his wife's *Last Poems* for the press. At first he avoided company, but gradually he accepted invitations more freely and began to move in society. Another collected edition of his poems was called for in 1863, but *Pauline* was not included. When his next book of poems, *Dramatis Personae* (1864)—including *Abt Vogler*, *Rabbi Ben Ezra*, *Caliban upon Setebos*, and *Mr. Sludge, "The Medium"*—reached two editions, it was clear that Browning had at last won a measure of popular recognition.

In 1868–69 he published his greatest work, *The Ring and the Book*, based on the proceedings in a murder trial in Rome in 1698. Grand alike in plan and execution, it was at once received with enthusiasm, and Browning was established as one of the most important literary figures of the day. For the rest of his life he was much in demand in London society. He spent his summers with friends in France, Scotland, or Switzerland or, after 1878, in Italy.

The most important works of his last years, when he wrote with great fluency, were long narrative or dramatic poems, often dealing with contemporary themes. While staying in Venice in 1889, Browning caught a cold, became seriously ill, and died on December 12. He was buried in Westminster Abbey.

CHARLOTTE BRONTË

(b. April 21, 1816, Thornton, Yorkshire, Eng.—d. March 31, 1855, Haworth, Yorkshire)

Charlotte Brontë was an English novelist best known for *Jane Eyre* (1847), a strong narrative of a woman in conflict with her natural desires and social condition. The novel gave new truthfulness to Victorian fiction.

Her father was Patrick Brontë (1777–1861), an Anglican clergyman. Irish-born, he had changed his name from the more commonplace Brunty. After serving in several parishes, he moved with his wife, Maria Branwell Brontë, and their six small children to Haworth amid the Yorkshire moors in 1820, having been awarded a rectorship there. Soon after, Mrs. Brontë and the two eldest children (Maria and Elizabeth) died, leaving the father to care for the remaining three girls—Charlotte,

Charlotte Brontë (1816–1855) achieved lasting fame as the author of Jane Eyre.

Emily, and Anne—and a boy, Patrick Branwell. Their upbringing was aided by an aunt, Elizabeth Branwell, who left her native Cornwall and took up residence with the family at Haworth.

In 1824 Charlotte and Emily, together with their elder sisters before their deaths, attended Clergy Daughters' School at Cowan Bridge, near Kirkby Lonsdale, Lancashire. The fees were low, the food unattractive, and the discipline harsh. Charlotte condemned the school (perhaps exaggeratedly) long years afterward in *Jane Eyre*, under the thin disguise of Lowood. Charlotte and Emily returned home in June 1825, and for more than five years the Brontë children learned and played there, writing and telling romantic tales for one another and inventing imaginative games played out at home or on the desolate moors.

In 1831 Charlotte was sent to Miss Wooler's school at Roe Head, near Huddersfield, where she stayed a year and made some lasting friendships. Her correspondence with one of her friends, Ellen Nussey, continued until her death, and has provided much of the current knowledge of her life. In 1832 she came home to teach her sisters but in 1835 returned to Roe Head as a teacher. The work, with its inevitable restrictions, was uncongenial to Charlotte. She fell into ill health and melancholia and in the summer of 1838 terminated her engagement.

In 1839 Charlotte declined a proposal from the Rev. Henry Nussey, her friend's brother, and some months later one from another young clergyman. At the same time Charlotte's ambition to make the practical best of her talents and the need to pay Branwell's debts urged her to spend some months as governess with the Whites at Upperwood House, Rawdon. Branwell's talents for writing and painting, his good classical scholarship, and his social charm had engendered high hopes for him; but he was fundamentally unstable, weak willed, and intemperate. He went from job to job and took refuge in alcohol and opium.

Meanwhile his sisters had planned to open a school together, which their aunt had agreed to finance. The plan would eventually fail, but in February 1842 Charlotte and Emily went to Brussels as pupils to improve their qualifications in French and acquire some German. The talent displayed by both brought them to the notice of Constantin Héger, a fine teacher and a man of unusual perception. After a brief trip home, Charlotte returned to Brussels as a pupil-teacher. She stayed there during 1843 but was lonely and depressed. Her friends had left Brussels, and Madame Héger appears to have become jealous of her. The nature of Charlotte's attachment to Héger and the degree to which she understood herself have been much discussed. She offered him an innocent but ardent devotion, but he tried to repress her emotions.

By 1846 Charlotte, Emily, and Anne were trying to place the three novels they had written. Charlotte failed to place *The Professor: A Tale* but had, however, nearly finished *Jane Eyre: An Autobiography*, begun in August 1846 in Manchester, where she was staying with her father, who had gone there for an eye operation. When Smith, Elder and Company, declining *The Professor*, declared themselves willing to consider a three-volume novel with more action and excitement in it, she completed and submitted it at once. *Jane Eyre* was accepted, published less than eight weeks later (on October 16, 1847), and had an immediate success, far greater than that of the books that her sisters published the same year. Central to its success is the fiery conviction with which it presented a thinking, feeling woman, craving for love but able to renounce it at the call of impassioned self-respect and moral conviction.

The months that followed were tragic ones. Branwell died in September 1848, Emily in December, and Anne in May 1849. Charlotte completed *Shirley: A Tale* in the empty parsonage, and it appeared in October. In the following years Charlotte went three times to London as the guest of her publisher; there she met the novelist William Makepeace Thackeray and sat for her portrait by George Richmond. She stayed in 1851 with the writer Harriet Martineau and also visited her future biographer, Mrs. Elizabeth Gaskell, in Manchester and entertained her at Haworth. *Villette* came out in January 1853. Meanwhile, in 1851, she had declined a third offer of marriage, this time from James Taylor, a member of Smith, Elder and Company. Her father's curate, Arthur Bell Nicholls (1817–1906), an Irishman, was her fourth suitor. It took some months to win her father's consent, but they were married on June 29, 1854. She began another book, *Emma*, of which some pages remain. Her pregnancy, however, was accompanied by exhausting sickness, and she died in 1855. Her first novel, *The Professor*, which is based on her experiences in Brussels, was published posthumously in 1857.

HENRY DAVID THOREAU

(b. July 12, 1817, Concord, Mass., U.S.—d. May 6, 1862, Concord)

The American essayist, poet, and practical philosopher Henry David Thoreau is renowned for having lived the doctrines of Transcendentalism as recorded in his masterwork, *Walden* (1854), and for having been a vigorous advocate of civil liberties, as evidenced in the essay "Civil Disobedience" (1849).

Thoreau entered Harvard University in 1833.

Graduating in the middle ranks of the class of 1837, he searched for a teaching job and secured one at his old grammar school in Concord. But he was no disciplinarian, and he resigned after two shaky weeks. A canoe trip that he and his brother John took along the Concord and Merrimack rivers in 1839 confirmed in him the opinion that he ought to be not a schoolmaster but a poet of nature.

Sheer chance made his entrance to writing easier, for he came under the benign influence of the essayist and poet Ralph Waldo Emerson, who had settled in Concord during Thoreau's sophomore year at Harvard. By the autumn of 1837, they were becoming friends. Emerson sensed in Thoreau a true disciple—that is, one with so much Emersonian self-reliance that he would still be his own man. Thoreau saw in Emerson a guide, a father, and a friend. With his magnetism Emerson attracted others to Concord. Out of their heady speculations and affirmatives came New England Transcendentalism.

In Emerson's company Thoreau's hope of becoming a poet looked not only proper but feasible. He wrote some poems—a good many, in fact—for several years. Captained by Emerson, the Transcendentalists started a magazine, *The Dial*; the inaugural issue, dated July 1840, carried Thoreau's poem *Sympathy* and his essay on the Roman poet Aulus Persius Flaccus.

The Dial published more of Thoreau's poems and then, in July 1842, the first of his outdoor essays, "Natural History of Massachusetts." Then followed more lyrics, such as *To the Maiden in the East*, and another nature essay, "A Winter Walk." *The Dial* ceased publication with the April 1844 issue, having published a richer variety of Thoreau's writing than any other magazine ever would.

By early 1845 Thoreau felt more restless than ever,

until he decided to take up an idea of a Harvard classmate who had once built a waterside hut in which one could loaf or read. In the spring Thoreau picked a spot by Walden Pond, a small lake south of Concord on land Emerson owned. Once settled, after building his home, he restricted his diet for the most part to the fruit and vegetables he found growing wild and the beans he planted. When not occupied with fishing, swimming, or rowing, he spent long hours observing and recording the local flora and fauna, reading, and writing.

Out of such activity and thought came *Walden*, a series of 18 essays describing Thoreau's experiment in basic living. Several of the essays provide his original perspective on the meaning of work and leisure and describe his experiment in living as simply and self-sufficiently as possible, while in others Thoreau describes the various realities of life at Walden Pond: his intimacy with the small animals he came in contact with; the sounds, smells, and look of woods and water at various seasons; the music of wind in telegraph wires. The physical act of living day by day at Walden Pond is what gives the book authority, while Thoreau's command of a clear, straightforward but elegant style helped raise it to the level of a literary classic.

Midway in his Walden sojourn Thoreau had spent a night in jail. On an evening in July 1846 he encountered Sam Staples, the constable and tax gatherer. Staples asked him amiably to pay his poll tax, which Thoreau had omitted paying for several years. He declined, and Staples locked him up. The next morning a still-unidentified lady, perhaps his aunt, Maria, paid the tax. Thoreau reluctantly emerged, did an errand, and then went huckleberrying. A single night, he decided, was enough to make his point that he could not support a government that endorsed slavery and waged an imperialist war against Mexico. His defense of the private, individual conscience against the expediency of the majority found expression in his most famous essay, "Civil Disobedience," which was first published in May 1849 under the title "Resistance to Civil Government."

When Thoreau left Walden in 1847, he passed the peak of his career. Slowly his Transcendentalism drained away as he became a surveyor in order to support himself. But as Thoreau became less of a Transcendentalist he became more of an activist—above all, a dedicated abolitionist. As much as anyone in Concord, he helped to speed fleeing slaves north on the Underground Railroad. He lectured and wrote against slavery. In the abolitionist John Brown he found a father figure beside whom Emerson paled. By now Thoreau was in poor health, and when Brown's raid on Harpers Ferry failed and he was hanged in 1859, Thoreau suffered a psychic shock that probably hastened his own death, apparently of tuberculosis.

EMILY BRONTË

(b. July 30, 1818, Thornton, Yorkshire, Eng.—d. Dec. 19, 1848, Haworth, Yorkshire)

Emily Brontë was an English novelist and poet who produced but one novel, *Wuthering Heights* (1847), a highly imaginative novel of passion and hate set on the Yorkshire moors.

Her father held a number of curacies: Hartshead-cum-Clifton, Yorkshire, was the birthplace of his elder daughters, Maria and Elizabeth (who died young), and nearby Thornton that of Emily and her siblings Charlotte, Patrick Branwell, and Anne. In 1820 the father became rector of Haworth, remaining there for the rest of his life.

After the death of their mother in 1821, the children were left very much to themselves in the bleak moorland rectory. The children were educated, during their early life, at home, except for a single year that Charlotte and Emily spent at the Clergy Daughters' School at Cowan Bridge in Lancashire. In 1835, when Charlotte secured a teaching position at Miss Wooler's school at Roe Head, Emily accompanied her as a pupil but suffered from homesickness and remained only three months. In 1838 Emily spent six exhausting months as a teacher in Miss Patchett's school at Law Hill, near Halifax, and then resigned.

To keep the family together at home, Charlotte planned to keep a school for girls at Haworth. In February 1842 she and Emily went to Brussels to learn foreign languages and school management. Although Emily pined for home and for the wild moorlands, it seems that in Brussels she was better appreciated than Charlotte. Her passionate nature was more easily understood than Charlotte's decorous temperament. In October, however, when her aunt died, Emily returned permanently to Haworth.

In 1845 Charlotte came across some poems by Emily, and this led to the discovery that all three sisters—Charlotte, Emily, and Anne—had written verse. A year later they published jointly a volume of verse, *Poems by Currer, Ellis and Acton Bell*, the initials of these pseudonyms being those of the sisters. The book of verse contained 21 of Emily's poems, and a consensus of later criticism has accepted the fact that Emily's verse alone reveals true poetic genius. The venture cost the sisters about £50 in all, and only two copies were sold.

By midsummer of 1847, Emily's *Wuthering Heights* and Anne's *Agnes Grey* had been accepted for joint publication by J. Cautley Newby of London, but publication of the three volumes was delayed until the appearance of their sister Charlotte's *Jane Eyre*, which was immediately and hugely successful. *Wuthering Heights*, when published in December 1847, did not fare well; critics were hostile, calling it too savage, too animal-like, and clumsy in construction. Only later did it come to be considered one of the finest novels in the English language. It is distinguished from other novels of the period by its dramatic and poetic presentation, its abstention from all comment by the author, and its unusual structure.

Soon after its publication, Emily's health began to fail rapidly. She had been ill for some time, but now her breathing became difficult, and she suffered great pain. She died of tuberculosis in December 1848. Emily was perhaps the greatest of the three Brontë sisters, but the record of her life is extremely meager, for she was silent and reserved and left no correspondence of interest. Her single novel darkens rather than solves the mystery of her spiritual existence.

Glossary

albatross: A large seabird.

allegory: The use of fictional figures and actions to symbolize truths or generalizations about human existence.

blasphemous: Showing disrespect to God or something holy.

convalesce: To recover health after an illness.

governess: A woman employed, usually in a private household, to teach someone's children and to act as their nanny.

laudanum: A preparation of the drug opium.

libel: To write and publish a false statement that represents someone in a negative way.

picaresque: Describes a story that involves a rogue or adventurer surviving mainly by his or her wits in a treacherous society.

platonic: Relating to a close relationship that is not romantic.

posthumous: Occurring after the death of a person.

Romanticism: An artistic movement of the late 18th century characterized by an emphasis on the individual, the subjective, the irrational, the imaginative, the personal, the spontaneous, the emotional, the visionary, and the transcendental.

satire: Something that makes fun of and shows the weaknesses of human nature.

serialize: To publish in parts over a period of time.

FOR MORE INFORMATION

BOOKS

Croy, Anita. *Charles Dickens.* New York, NY: Lucent Press, 2020.

Croy, Anita. *Jane Austen*. New York, NY: Lucent Press, 2020.

Lewis, Aura. *Spectacular Sisters: Amazing Stories of Sisters from Around the World.* New York, NY: Quill Tree Books, 2021.

Poe, Edgar Allan. *Selected Works of Edgar Allan Poe*. San Diego, CA: Canterbury Classics, 2020.

WEBSITES

Academy of American Poets
poets.org/poet/edgar-allan-poe
Read more biographical information about Edgar Allan Poe and find links to some of his most famous poems.

All Poetry
allpoetry.com/Robert-Browning
Read about the life of Robert Browning and listen to or read his poetry.

Charles Dickens Museum
dickensmuseum.com/
Learn more about Charles Dickens through the Charles Dickens Museum in London, England, which is located in one of his former homes.

Poetry Foundation
www.poetryfoundation.org/poets/john-keats
This site offers biographical information about John Keats and a selection of his poetry.

INDEX